COPYWRITE © 2018

By Rachelle Munson

The Starfish Portrait Book

Dedicated to my mother & father,
Ginger Munson & Richard Munson.
Also, my wonderful grandmother,
Isabella Sapone, who lived to be 107.

Copyrights

Thank you for viewing!

A special thank you for creative commons images from pixabay.com, stocksnap.io, & the last photo taken by Paul Shaffner.

www.ingramcontent.com/pod-product-compliance
Lightning Source LLC
Chambersburg PA
CBHW060800270326
41926CB00002B/43